LETTERS to the EARTH

First published 2005 *by*
Veritas Publications
7/8 Lower Abbey Street
Dublin 1
Ireland
Email publications@veritas.ie
Website www.veritas.ie

ISBN 1 85390 881 9

10 9 8 7 6 5 4 3 2 1

A catalogue record for this book is available from the British Library.

Acknowledgements
Some of this material has appeared in a different format in *Ireland's Own*. The author wishes to thank the editors and publishers of the magazine.

Printed in the Republic of Ireland by Betaprint Dublin

Veritas books are printed on paper made from the wood pulp of managed forests. For every tree felled, at least one tree is planted, thereby renewing natural resources.

CONTENTS

Dedication

Remembering my two good friends,
Sweep and Sooty.

INTRODUCTION

When I was young, I think I discovered a simple truth. Nature can be a force for good in our lives. It can touch us with its beauty and its quiet, its sheer diversity too. I began to appreciate that we live in a world where nothing is ordinary. Every tree and bird and flower has a magic, a meaning, an essence of its own.

The bond with nature was part of the fabric of everyday life, but so much has changed of late. We are encroaching more and more on nature's space and yet paradoxically we are living our lives at a further and further remove from it. It is as if we have begun to believe that we are separate from nature, detached from it, that we can do with it what we will and that it makes no difference at all. The truth is that for all our foolish notions of superiority we too are part of the fabric. We too are a thread in the shining web of earth. If we diminish the least part of it, we diminish ourselves. The fish and the flowers, the birds and the animals have just as much right to be here as any of humankind. If the time is short, as it is, then surely the lives of all living things deserve a gentleness of touch, a respect, a reverence too.

Nature is a myriad of things. It is a hundred different things all at once. It is brightness and joy, reflection and calm. It puts a value on slowness in a world that makes rushing a virtue.

It is the fox and the lark and the crest of the ocean wave. It is the gorse and the heather and the promise of summer. It is winter shining. More than these, it is the very breath of earth itself, the green grass warm and growing. Nature is part of what we are, part of our humanity, and if we turn our backs on it, then it is we who are the lesser for it.

I am writing this in spring and the robin is nesting again in the mossy bank by the wayside, the primroses gathered around her. The boughs of the ash are greening and leafing above her. I wish her good fortune and brightness; I wish her the joy of long summer days. I am never happier than when I see her peeping from the moss. She is the brightness of earth: the joy of all that nature gives; beauty and stillness and more.

JANUARY

Dear Earth,

I write to you as I would my dearest friend, for that is how I think of you. You have always been my joy and delight, my wellspring of hope for tomorrow. You bring me simple pleasures. A new year, new hopes, new beginnings, but I am conscious again of the passage of time.

I love to look up at the starry sky, the 'full starred heaven that winter sees'. It fills me with mystery and wonder but it gives me perspective too. It makes me think how small we are, how minute in the great cosmos of planets and stars. It gives me a sense of your worth, dear friend, star among stars, beautiful planet green and blue. You are a jewel of the heavens with your crowded woods and teeming seas, your mysteries of land and ocean. Just looking at the sky renews my faith in you, my hope in you, my trust.

I, in turn, renew my pledge to you, my promise to cherish and respcct, to love you all of my days. I don't know when I began to look up at the sky. All I know is that I was still a child and I am glad of it. In recent times space missions have given us glimpses of other planets and stars. They have been our windows to other worlds. We have, for instance, seen something of the strange, alien beauty of Saturn's moon, Titan: landscapes with boulders beneath a faint orange sky. These images merely add to the sense of mystery, reminding us as they do of the vastness of space. They remind us too of the beauty of our own planet with all its riches of life and colour, its sheer diversity too: trees and flowers and birds, the rhythm of raindrops falling.

I love to hear the curlews call along the river, their calling soft and lonely in the still of the silver night. The river is the river of dreams, forever free and flowing, full of echoes of brightness. My father loved the river and the salmon, the mythical magical salmon that brought the river to life. They were living silver, echoes of wise men and druids, a legacy worthy of praise. Finn got his wisdom from the Salmon of Knowledge, the Bradan Feasa. Still he was jealous of the lovers Diarmaid and Grannia. When they were on the run, they headed south and west till they came to the river Laune. They caught a salmon there, cooked it on one side of the river and ate it on the other. This was the advice of their protector, Aonghus the God of Love. And we read in our books at school how heroes caught salmon in style. They put berries of rowan on hooks and then made a cast with a line. That was a neat trick but the rowan was magic, the favourite tree of the druids. There are plenty of rowan trees here, plenty of berries to shine in the glow of the autumn sun.

The fishermen loved the river, not just the banks and the fishing places, but the birds and the otters too. There are herons and shelduck and swans and of course the lapwings in winter. The herons fish in the long-legged pools; they love the slow-moving stream. I have seen the lapwings gathered at the river's edge at dusk. The light was fading then, the pale orange glow reflected in the stillness of the water. The reeds were orange and rusted and brown, the lapwings set like dark silhouettes against the tide. They looked almost drowsy there till a few of them took to the air and flashed their wings in flight. It was magical to hear their bright 'pee-wits' with the outlines of the mountains rising dark across the sky.

I was walking by the river another day. The tide was glassy and calm, reflections of the mountains shining below, their snowy peaks in reflex. Suddenly the skies overhead were filled with wonderful, bugling calls and when I looked up there was a flock of whooper swans going past. I was filled with wonder at their strangeness and their beauty. The whiteness of their wings had echoes, such echoes of the gleaming wastelands of the north, the frozen wastes of ice and snow that stretch far and away. I was spellbound a while. Their flight was majestic; it would be hard to imagine anything more beautiful. They called to one another time and again, their bugling calls filling the skies, though their wings were without the rhythmic throb of their mute counterparts. There are always swans on the river, but these were strangers, strangers from the north, everything about them wild and beautiful and free. They set me to thinking again. I felt sure their kind was seen by many a fisherman down through the years. There were a great many boats on the river then, draft net fishing for salmon. There must have been days when the men were making their hauls that they heard the bugles overhead, the wild bugling calls of the swans. And maybe they stopped and looked and listened. And maybe they stood in wonder just like me. The swans were touchstones of beauty, dear friend, the keepers of memory too. The thought of them stayed with me a very long time. I looked for them again, but did not find them. Maybe it was just as well; magic like theirs does not happen every day and I have my memories still. Time and again I picture them, their magical wings outspread, the river shining below. They were the voice of the snows, they were the snows come to life.

The brent geese come from the northlands too. I love to watch them feed in tidal waters on a crisp, cold winter's day. At a distance they look small and dark, mostly dark grey and black with white undertails. They feed by paddling in the beds of eel grass or by dipping their heads and upending in deeper water. They are never alone; they are always in flocks together and their call has a kind of rolling throaty sound to it. It is only when they take to the air that their gleaming white undertails are seen and I look up again. I look up at my friends, the brent, bringing me joys from a far place. And when the

rains came, the swans and the shelduck forsook the river for the bright shining pools in the fields. But I went back to the river again, the dark waves grey and wild. I was thinking of the time not so long ago when I saw two whiskered heads in the water: two young otters having games in the grey swell all around them. They curled and curved and rolled and wrestled. It was not a postcard scene. There was no blue tide and no bright hills and yet there was something strangely elemental about them. It was as if they belonged to the river and it belonged to them. They were the essence of nature and when they came ashore they played again like buoyant children in the seaweed on the slip. I stood and looked, still filled with pleasure.

Day fades. The night comes again with the moon and the stars and the frost, the grasses starched and silvered, the tangled hedges hoary too. The lonely calls of the curlews echo far and away, the peewits feeding in the moonlight. I think of the river sleeping but what its dreams are no one knows. There are things it keeps secret, things that are only hinted at under the light of the moon. Dear earth, my heart is always happy for sharing in your beauty, your wildness a while. My heart is wiser for sensing the mystery of winter skies. Dear friend, you are the sphere of wonder, the storehouse of days and nights and seasons. Let me be glad of each one; let me make the most of them all.

Until I write again,

Always your friend,

Patrick

FEBRUARY

Dear Earth,

I remember a woman looking at me wryly when I was buying a book one day. I think she was wondering why anyone in their right mind would want to buy a book all about hedgehogs. There are days in winter, grey days of mist and drizzle, when I think it would be nice to be a hedgehog, to fall asleep with blackberries and wake again with snowdrops. Many hedgehogs keep going until November, however, though almost all are thought to wake up sometime in February, the first month of spring, the month of renewal and rebirth. When making their nests they gather leaves and grass and find a safe place, under the roots of a tree or in bramble patches. Here they comb and re-comb the leaves until they overlap and create a waterproof haven, giving the hedgehog good insulation against the winter cold. If the nest is made beneath the hedge however, the occupant may be at risk from farm machinery, especially in the case where fields are enlarged and hedges destroyed.

A young fella once told me that he wouldn't be surprised if he met a badger coming up my garden path. It was his way of telling me that my shrubs were all overgrown and wild, but I took the mention of the badger as a great compliment. 'I should be so lucky', I thought to myself. Most forms of wildlife, including badgers and hedgehogs, are not very fond of picture-book gardens. They like a bit of wildness here and there and hedgehogs, in particular, are amongst the world's most effective natural pesticides. They eat everything from insects, slugs and snail to earwigs and beetles. Another point in their favour is that ladybirds do not figure in their diet at all and as everyone knows, the ladybird gets rid of large numbers of aphids and greenfly which damage growing plants. Hibernation and sleep are not one and the same, but when I caught sight of a hedgehog in his nest under a tangle of climbers by the wall I couldn't help wondering what he was dreaming of. Was he dreaming of gardens with a little bit of wild in them, gardens full of butterflies, flowers and birds, where pesticides and insecticides are not the order of the day? There are alternatives to slug pellets too: spiky suckers from roses, nettles, brambles, even sharp crushings of wood, all can make a painful barrier to keep slugs and snails at bay. And what could be nicer than to find a hedgehog at rest under vines or woodbines or other climbers on a summer day. I think if I had a motto it would be 'a garden with a hedgehog is a good garden'.

In Irish tradition it was good to see a hedgehog moving about at this time of year, all the more so if he were seen on St Brigid's Day. It was said that he forsook the warmth of his winter nest to make a check on the weather. If the weather was good he stayed out, which meant that the days ahead would be mild. The hedgehog giving up his nest to make his own little weather forecast: it is a lovely thought, but then those were the days when satellite charts were unheard of and maybe the hedgehog's way of doing things is not without merit still. I was never very good at geography at school. When it came to filling in maps, I was always moving things around. Apart from a bit about climate, however, there was very little about nature or the countryside and we can learn so much from nature, from creatures such as the hedgehog and their instinctive bond with the rhythm of the seasons. Winter is a time for reading, or at least it was. Our world, it seems, has become mesmerised by the spell of technology. We are held spellbound not just by television, but by computers, picture phones and more. Virtual reality is seen as the pinnacle of achievement and yet despite all this technical wizardry, we have not yet managed to replicate the beauty of trees and flowers and birds. Virtual reality does not even come close to the magic of such things, but then why would we want

to replace them when nature does it so perfectly for us? In his poem, 'When I consider everything that grows', Shakespeare reflected on both the perfection and the transience of nature. He was right in one thing: nature is perfection and the fact that it is so short-lived, makes it all the more wonderful still. There is nothing more magical than to find the first snowdrops, the first crocuses in the garden on a crisp, cold day. The snowdrop, especially the most popular variety *Galanthus nivalis*, has long been a favourite in Irish country gardens large and small. An account of an old country garden in Kildare in the eighteenth century, for instance, describes it as being in the antique taste with borders of yew and holly and a jessamine tree, probably jasmine, by the parlour window: 'Beyond it an orchard white with snowdrops in the spring'. The orchard would have been the perfect place for them, for they are easily naturalised in grass.

As everyone knows, the outer petals are white, but the inner ones are tipped with green. It is this very simplicity that gives the snowdrop its special appeal. There is nothing showy about it, nothing ostentatious. It is almost shy, retiring in character. Despite their apparent fragility, however, snowdrops are strong. It is something of a miracle that they bloom at all when the mountain peaks are capped with snow, dazzling white in the winter sun. The robin warbles on the leafless boughs, but he too has a cold, ruffled look about him. The snowdrops, however, have a secret of their own. They are the secret keepers. They can flower so early because they store food in their bulbs. This means that they do not have to look for nourishment in the still frozen ground. Even when snow falls in the garden and the boughs are dredged with white, the little flowers keep blooming. The daffodils are sleeping still, the wild bluebells the same, but the snowdrops brave the cold and snow to tell of spring again.

The flowers are followed by little green capsules which have many seeds. The seeds often drop close to the parent plant which leads to the development of small colonies. It is lovely to come across a little cluster of snowdrops in damp, deciduous woodland. The branches of beech and oak are leafless, but the snowdrops remind us that spring is stirring again. They are not only beautiful in themselves, they are heralds of things to come, a promise of brighter days. Dear earth, thank you for all the magical simplicity of snowdrops, for the reassurance that despite all the damage we have done to you, the earth flowers and blooms again in spring. If we could find someone who knew nothing of the beauty of flowers, and show them a snowdrop bulb, a simple little snowdrop bulb in the palm of their hand, would they ever believe that it had such beauty in it? Would they not think of the nodding white flowers as miracles, not just those that grow in gardens, but especially those that grow in the wild, for that is what they are, a miracle of miracles.

And yet so many of us barely give them a second glance. We look but we do not see.

Snowdrops are the music of spring; tunes for a snowy day. Their theme is renewal, rebirth, regeneration and if there is not a message of hope for humankind in that, then we have surely lost something of our sense of wonder, our sense of the marvellous, the magical in nature. Like the spiny hedgehog, the snowdrops are reminders that winter is over and spring is at hand. No more than the hedgehog they like the freedom of the wild; they like to be unrestricted, unconfined. They make me happy when I see them for I know in my heart of hearts that it will not be long till the birds are singing again.

Until I write again,

Always your friend,

Patrick

MARCH

Dear Earth,

The days are getting brighter and the birds have begun to sing. Of all the singers in the hedge the blackbird was very much a favourite with the ancient Irish. His song is mentioned time and again in the myths and sagas and there is no great wonder in that. His singing is wild, melodious and full of content. Whenever I hear him, I am filled with joy. Of course, there are many reasons why birds sing, mainly to establish territory. This is especially important in the breeding season, when the male also has hopes of impressing a partner with the beauty of his song. It is as if the song, the magical song, is at the very heart of creation, nurturing, sustaining and making it new. Still, I like to think that he sings for the sheer pleasure of it too. After all, he has reasons to be happy: not just the lengthening days and the prospect of fine weather but so much more besides. The yellows of buttercups, celandines and daffodils in damp meadow and marsh and all the wild places; the building, the making, the smoothing and shaping of the wonderful well of the nest; the drinking from pools, and – when the young are fledged at last – the promise of fruits in summer gardens, raspberries and strawberries and currants and cherries. After that again, the taste of fallen apples in the orchard; one of the great pleasures of autumn for the blackbird and his kind.

When I hear him sing, it makes me think how lucky he is. He is not weighed down with the baggage of the past. The time that is gone is not a burden to him. Nor does he fret too much about the future. He takes each day, each moment, as it comes and the more I think about it, the more I think there is a lot to be said for it. Sometimes in our human world, we are slow to let go of the past. Maybe we should take our lead from the blackbird and rejoice with him at winter's passing, remembering what is good in our lives and looking to the future with hope.

The English essayist, Joseph Addison, had the right idea when it came to blackbirds: 'I value my garden more for being full of blackbirds than of cherries and very freely give them fruit for their song.' The anonymous ninth-century writer who wrote so vividly of 'the little bird whistling from a bright yellow bill' would have agreed with him, I'm sure. Apart from the sheer beauty of their song, one of the things I like about blackbirds is that they don't all sound the same. They are not afraid to try out variations of their own. I remember walking by an old ruined abbey. It was a fine spring day, a blackbird at rest on one of the slanted sides of the gable. His song was wonderfully wild and bright, but very distinctive too. Some of the notes were decidedly different to those produced by Black, the resident blackbird in my garden. The abbey and its environs can be a sombre place on rainy days, but it was lovely to hear the blackbird sing with such delight. There was or never could be a more powerful symbol of hope.

There is something else about the blackbird's song that intrigues me, and not just his song, but the song of all the birds. Their song, though fleeting, is enduring too. It is the selfsame song that has been heard by generations before us, the selfsame song that has given them joy and comfort and hope. It is in that way an inextricable part of the human emotion and experience, a part that enriches and enhances and gives meaning to our world. The singers may be different but the song is still the same, which makes it all the more pressing that we should pass it on in all its unspoiled beauty to those who come after us. After all, what is there to rival the blackbird's song. Yellow-billed, golden-voiced blackbird. Could anyone imagine the woods and groves without him?

It is the time of year when the first of the dog violets begin to bloom, surely one of the most attractive plants of the shady bank or the fringes of the wood. The rich violet blueflowers as well as the heart-shaped leaves give it a special appeal. While thrushes sing for much of the year, most blackbirds do not begin to sing till late February or so. The lateness of the start merely adds to its magic, however; the song having, as one expert put it, 'a mellowness and contentment above all others'. In a lovely poem called 'Thirteen Ways of Looking at a Blackbird', the American poet Wallace Stevens wondered which he liked best, the beauty of the blackbird's song or the memory of it afterwards. I know the feeling well and as the days get brighter and warmer, the blackbird will sing not just in the morning but late in the evening too. Then the sun will be a fire in the west, his song a celebration of the close of another day. Of course the blackbird loves the dripping leaves and hedges too, the rhythm of the raindrops like music all around him.

The longer evenings mean that I can do a bit more cycling and there is nothing lovelier than to cycle through the countryside on a fine spring evening. Then the skies are bright, and the very earth itself smells of the richness of greenness and growth, the hedges greening too. In the past there was always a bond with nature, a bond with trees and birds and flowers, but in our world today, so many people, even those who live in the countryside, live at a remove from it. Their view of the world is framed by the car window, so that much of the beauty, the colour, the diversity passes them by. There is no time for rejoicing in detail: the beauty of buds unfolding, the soft murmur of the stream. Those who walk or cycle, on the other hand, (and the Victorians, for all their flaws, were great lovers of both) can stop a while and look in wonder. They can reclaim the miracle and make it their own, the miracle of buds and leaves and greening hedges.

This, too, is the time for planting and sowing, the scattering of seeds, and at a time when there is so much talk of mass production and economies of scale, it is nice to think that there are some at least who have gone back to the old ways, nature's ways. Organic farming is sometimes thought of as some revolutionary new concept, but is it really? In many ways the idea has always been there. It is all about showing respect for nature and for you, dear friend, the earth, giving something back instead of always taking. It is no more than man in harmony with soil and season. The organic farmers of today may be pioneers in one sense, but in another they are simply following in the footsteps of so many who have gone before. The ways of nature are patient and fruitful and slow and that in itself is a lesson in a world that demands so much so quickly. Nature takes its own time and maybe we should too: maybe we should learn the virtue of patience from the trees and the flowers and the fruits:

Nor shall he know when loud March blows
thro' slanting snows her fanfare shrill,
blowing to flame the golden cup
of many an upset daffodil.

Francis Ledwidge

I think if I were given the choice of having just one flower in my garden, I would choose the daffodil for it is the daffodil more than any other that encapsulates all the wonder and joy of spring. Down through the years, it has inspired the poets time and time again. I have even tried my hand at writing a poem or two for the daffodil myself. Whenever I look at the daffodils I think of a line from one of the old Irish sagas. In the line, Emer says to Cuchulainn: 'What is new is beautiful, what is familiar stale. The unknown honoured, the known neglected'. All too often there is something of this in our attitude to the daffodil. We see them so often and in so many places that we begin to take them for granted. We think of them as commonplace, ordinary, and yet nothing could be further from the truth. The daffodil is the very essence of spring. Could anyone imagine a spring without them, imbued as they are with all the hope and promise of the season. They bring to mind all the beauty around us: birdsong and brightness and lambs in the fields. If only we could look at them with the eyes of first looking, with a sense of wonder. Their golden trumpets too are a foil for the bareness of the boughs, though it will not be long till the sticky chestnut buds disclose their silky greens. Sometimes the daffodils are perfectly still. Sometimes they ripple in waves when the breeze comes whispering by. It is as if the daffodils and the breeze are in league with one another, as if they have a pact of their own.

Maybe it is a foolish thought but I always think

of daffodils as companionable flowers. It is very rarely that you see one of its own, a solitary daffodil all alone. No, they come in great sweeps or rushes, flanking avenues, boreens and byways, as if they revel in the nearness of friends. In a way they offer the same fellowship, the same companionship to humankind, the likes of you and me. I for one am glad of my yellow companions when the days are cold and bright. Then the blackbird is busy too, moulding and shaping the well of his nest in the greening hedge. Dear earth, thank you for daffodils and blackbirds and all the joys of the season, the beauty given breath, the hope reborn, and skies like a prayer at evening.

Until I write again,

Always your friend,

Patrick

APRIL

Dear Earth,

The water came bubbling up through the road and though it looked like a leak at first someone said it might be a natural spring. There was a kind of mystery about it and in a way there was no great wonder in that. The ancient Irish attached a sense of mystery to many of their springs and wells, not just praising their beauty but giving them a sacred character. In one story, Oisín went in search of water for a feast, coming at last to the white-rimmed well of Uisneach. There he saw eight beautiful salmon 'clothed in their diversely coloured hues, the intricacy of the place being such that they needed not to fear anything.' Oisín picked eight sprigs of watercress and eight of brooklime, then scooping up some of the salmon with a pail, he put the cress and the brooklime floating on top. The image of the well is a very vivid one and reflects the reverence of the Celts for such places. Another member of the Fianna, Caoilte, recited a poem in praise of a well, rejoicing in its beauty and fame. The arum lilies grew around it, 'the dappled red-bellied fawns' coming there to drink. The well was more than just a source of water, it was all about healing, fertility, purity too. The water that bubbled up through the road turned out to be a leak after all, but still it was nice to wonder for a while.

I have to admit that I did not like to see all that precious water spilling wastefully away. I thought of all the good it could do in the places of arid seasons where no rain falls at all from year to year. We are always complaining about the rain but where would we be without it? It makes the fields and hedges green: it gives the birds their bathing places. And yet it is almost as if we have grown comfortable with waste, as if we see nothing wrong in it at all. We see virtue in the disposable, the throwaway, when it would serve us better to make things last, repairing, restoring, giving new leases of life. Or is it that we cannot accept that your resources are finite, dear earth? Is it that we think they will go on forever? We have to show them respect to make the right choices too, looking to the renewable, the sustainable, instead of the expedient. Thinking only of what is good for you, for what is good for you will be good for us too in the long run. Giving back the sacred to the water and the well, the purity of seas and skies, all precious things we take for granted every day. Very often in the past there was no choice but to make things last. Now that we have choices, let us think and choose wisely.

There are few scenes in nature which can rival the beauty of wild bluebells in springtime. They carpet the woods with their dark and inky blues, softening to hazier tones as they stream far and away beneath the trees. There the light comes pouring down and the songs of birds are heard among the branches. No wonder then that my old Victorian flower book waxes lyrical about the bluebell, contrasting its rich extravagant blues with the paler tints of primrose and the like. The writer of the book was right about something else too. He wrote that the spectacle of wild bluebells, once seen and enjoyed would never be forgotten. As the poet puts it 'The bluebell lights the copse, the primrose paves the glen'. Perhaps not surprisingly bluebells were seen as emblems of hope in Irish traditioon. This found expression in the lovely old saying: 'Bluebells in deep woods are found.'

I woke up Good Friday morning last to find a stranger passing by my window. I had seen his kind in the fields before, but never so close to the window as this. I was honoured by his coming, though I marvelled at the strangeness of it too. It wasn't just his beauty, it was the way that he seemed so relaxed. It was as if he had passed the way a hundred times before and I had never seen him. I was filled with delight, for what could be nicer than to see a pheasant go by my window first thing in the morning? I revelled in the splendour of his glossy green head and in all of those coppery tints shimmering and shining with light. It made me think of all the times I had seen his kind in the woods: pheasants rocketing skywards, explosions of copper and crowing but there he was, walking slowly past. It was lovely to see him so close, to see how the light played games with the metallic sheen of his feathers.

Despite the fame of their 'towering flight' as their upward flurry is sometimes called, pheasants far prefer to run and crouch in cover. They spend most of their time on the ground, where they eat seeds and grain, and roots and leaves. The female is not at all as colourful as her male counterpart. Yellow-brown with dark speckles and a somewhat shorter tail, she makes a very simple nest in cover in the ground, very occasionally in other places, where she lays up to sixteen olive-brown eggs. The chicks which are hatched in three to four weeks are beautifully marked and can fly in a matter of two weeks. I kept thinking it was lovely to have such a visitor on such a glorious morning.

We went to the sea soon after. The mountains hazy soft and blue, the tide a wild and glittering blue, the sun glistening in lines that seemed to go on forever, the waves spilling light on the shore, so that it was hard to tell where the sea ended and the sky began. We walked to the old tower and beyond, the tower half sinking in the sand but still sturdy enough in its way. As we made our way back, the sound of the waves was rhythmic and strong, the blue rhythms of the sea. The larks were singing in the sand dunes. I put a few shells in my pocket, keepsakes to remind me of a beautiful day.

It is the season of leafing and greening and I am struck again by the magic of the leaves, not just their beauty but their sheer diversity too; the simple and the compound, the narrow and the broad, the lobed and the pinnate and the palmate too. Of course, we don't need any of these terms to appreciate their beauty, to sense the magic in their fabulous textures and colours: smooth or glossy or downy; myriads of limes and greens, light and dark and darker still. Leaves, of course, have a very special and important role to play: they fan out to the sunlight with the green chlorophyll inside them making food for the tree. I have to admit I love ash, the familiar ash, their big black buds unfurling to disclose their marvellous greens. Some trees like the larch, another favourite of mine, have separate male and female flowers which change their colour from rosy red to crimson. It is these which develop into the fabulous cones, the cones maturing in the autumn or the following spring but remaining on the trees for up to ten years or more.

The more I think about these things the more magical they seem. First the flowers burgeoning from the wood, then the pollen carried in the wind and finally the cones themselves. Creation renewed in the boughs of the larch. The needles of the larch will in time turn yellow, the leaves of its broad-leaved neighbours with the promise of colour too: the magical tints of autumn.

Dear earth, let me be grateful for the beauty of trees and leaves, for ash and larch and willow, for the magic of the greening hedge and all the birds at their song.

Until I write again,

Always your friend,

Patrick

MAY

Dear Earth,

The fields are warm and green with grasses. The two donkeys, two best friends are grazing in the buttercup garden. There is a feeling of warmth and companionship about them, the buttercups yellow and golden. The buttercup garden is a long narrow place and yet the donkeys do not complain. They are happy with their lot. They have all the room in the world. I have seen them with buttercups and grasses in their mouths; they love the taste of summer, the joy of summer days.

I found an old frying pan and used it as a feeder for the hens, filling it with the grain that they like so much. The hens are Rhode Island hens, their warm reds and browns adding their own touch of colour to the scene, but before I opened their door every morning I placed the pan in the yard. The robins came as usual for their own little helping. At first they were intrigued by the frying pan but they were soon hopping into it, pecking away at their leisure. I had to smile when I saw them there.

Robins in a frying pan. Who'd have thought they'd feel so at home, but they did. They were not alone however. Sparrows chirped in the fuchsias and finches fluttered in the old apple boughs. They liked the frying pan too, but whereas they seemed to skirt round the edges, the robins were always at the centre. I tried in vain last year to find the robins' nest. I looked in the privet hedge and in the mossy bank by the road. I had seen them there before and I knew that when it came to choosing a nest site, they were fond of hollows of all kinds. I looked in the spotted laurel and in the hedge nearby but I found no trace of the elusive nest. Still the lilacs were in bloom and the scent was delicious. It would have been a lovely combination, lilacs and robins together in a little nook of their own, but if the nest was there, I could not find it.

It was strange that I should find it this year when I was not looking for it at all. I set about cutting the ivy from an old apple tree when I found it wedged in the very fork of the tree. It was magical to see it there, a wonderful weave of mosses set so neatly, so compactly, into the fork. It was almost as if the tree were hugging it, embracing it, keeping it safe, as if the tree were a protective spirit. The notion was not as fanciful as it seemed at first. Our ancestors, the Celts, believed in such things; they believed that their gods, their spirits, were everywhere in nature, in the woods and in the rivers, in the very land itself.

Luckily, I had begun to cut the ivy from a side branch so that the nest was still protected.

Needless to say, I gave up my cutting at once and looked in wonder at the eggs, five tiny eggs. They were beautiful things, white but speckled with light red spots. The finding of the nest struck the deepest of chords. It wasn't just the evocation of memories, memories of when I was a boy I searched in the fields and lanes for the nests of blackbird and robin and thrush. No, there was no more to it than that. It was the thought of creation still going on, there in that quiet nook, there in the arms of the tree. It was a magical thought and one that filled me with joy. It made me think again of the resilience of nature, the power of rebirth, renewal, regeneration, all of which goes on so quietly we take it for granted sometimes. We make no wonder of it at all. And yet if we stopped to think, we would see that every nest in every tree is a wonder, a miracle of eggs and mosses and new life stirring again. Already I am looking forward, looking forward to joy. It will not be long till the speckled young are hopping in the garden, till they feel at home among the roses and sweet williams and lupins too, the protective calls of their parents keeping them from danger. It is lovely to wake in the morning and hear the birds at their song. The first robin begins to sing about an hour before sunrise. It is only as the darkness begins to fade and dissolve that the blackbirds and thrushes, and later still the warblers and finches join in. There was one, a man of birds, who wrote that there was plenty of singing in the rain from the robin at that hour of the morning. It is almost as if they anticipate the brightness and the light, as if they know it is coming, that dawn is on the way.

I remember as a child the blackbird singing in the boughs of the sycamore just outside my window. He was closest of them all and I pictured him there all black and shining among the leaves, his magical song pouring from his yellow bill. I have heard the cuckoo, the voice of summer in the woods again. As I stood and listened I felt a great rejoicing. He was coming again, coming home for summer. He made me think of all my childhood summers, when happiness and freedom were but one emotion. Then there was paddling in the river and running in the meadows and never thinking of time at all. I pictured him there among the trees, all grey and barred as he made his soft cuckoos. He made the herons restless but I was glad of his coming. He made me feel young again.

Dear Earth, thank you for all the gifts of May, for beech leaves green and soft as silk, for pine trees shedding pollen, for chestnut spikes that glisten in the rain. Thank you for bluebells and buttercups and cuckoo flowers that love the meadows green and damp. I love to walk at evening time, the hawthorn hedges bright along the way. Their flowers are like the snows of summer, scenting the air in the still of the evening. And then the blackbird starts to sing, his singing wild, melodious, content. He is the

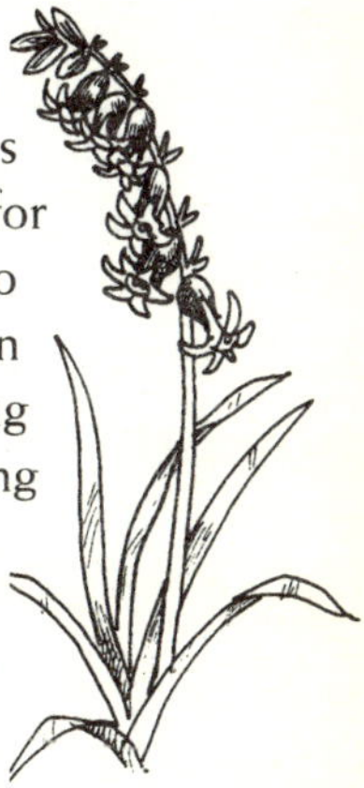

voice of contentment. The light from the west is mystical and for a while it seems that the light and the song are one and the same, seamless, beautiful and bright. The blackbird's song makes me imagine. I wonder what it would be like to be him, perched among the branches, the light of the evening falling in folds around him. He has reasons to be happy and he knows it. He has his mate and his young and all the joys of summer, the sun and the shade and the bright pools for bathing. His philosophy is simple but profound. He lives at one with you, dear friend, and I long to do the same. He thinks of you as a garden, a garden of beautiful things.

When I stop to listen I am certain of this much at least: there is truth in the blackbird's song.

Until I write again,

Always your friend,

Patrick

JUNE

Dear Earth,

This is the time of the foxgloves, the fairy thimbles. They parade on grassy banks but I have them in the garden too. I love to see their purple thimbles spill with rain, or to hear the honey bees hum with pleasure inside them. The colour of the fairy thimbles is rich and royal, a fitting colour for the fairy race. Their touch as soft as silk, the downy leaves softer still. They say that foxgloves are good for the heart. That may be so but they are good for the soul, the spirit too. They are the beauty of summer, the treasure of long summer days. I know that I am richer for them.

I love the quiet of country lanes. There is a little pool, no more than a dip, a hollow in a waste place. It is hardly worth a second glance, some would say, but for me it is a place of enchantment. I call it 'The Pool of Four Thrushes'. It is a favourite bathing place of the birds, especially the thrushes. I saw four thrushes bathing there in the drowsy heat of the afternoon. How they relished the coolness of the water, wetting, dripping, soaking through their feathers. It was as if they thought there was magic in every drop. I marvelled at the little speckled birds; they were magic for me, making the pool more beautiful still. It was as if it were a sacred place, a place for sustaining song. It was nurturing all those silver notes that pour from the birds on warm June days. It was as if the water and the thrushes and the song were as one. Without the water, there would be no thrushes: without the thrushes there would be no song. It made me think of the interdependence of things. We are all part of your fabric, dear Earth. If we hurt any part of it, then we are all hurt, we are all diminished in some way. I could never imagine summer without the magic of the thrush's song, the beauty of their speckled breasts among the branches. That is why I too pay homage at the pool, 'The Pool of Four Thrushes'. It reminds me of what is important and what is not; it is a way of honouring you, dear friend.

The poet Robert Browning celebrated the magic of the thrush's song in his poetry:

> That's the wise thrush that sings each song twice over
> Lest you should think that he never could recapture
> The first fine careless rapture.

Meanwhile, Gerard Manley Hopkins conveyed something of the beauty of the thrush's eggs. He wrote 'Thrush's eggs look like little low heavens'.

Anyone who has ever had the pleasure of seeing a thrush's nest with eggs will readily identify with these sentiments. As one old bird book of mine puts it: 'the blue of the thrush's egg is like no other.' Nature is full of richness and diversity and there is no more powerful expression of this than the beauty of thrush's eggs, the nest itself set in sprays of wild woodbine or caught in the fork of an elder tree.

It may be a foolish thought, a childish thought, but I have never seen a thrush counting pennies. We, on the other hand, burden ourselves with things, possessions. We make them our gods. I love the thrushes and the pool. I love the woodbine spilling scent in the lazy afternoon and the harts tongue ferns all dark and green and glossy by the way. I was sitting on a stone one evening, ribbons of fire painted away to the west. There were ash trees around with two old stone pillars flanking a gateway. Some years ago, the gates were taken down for repair. A stone was dislodged in the process, leaving a gap just beneath the cap of one of the pillars. As I sat and watched, I saw a little bird flitting purposefully in and out of the space. I soon recognised him as a blue tit, in Irish *Meantan gorm*, in Latin *Parus Caeruleus*. Even the very words have a lyrical ring to them, wonderfully evocative as they are, of the fabulous blue crown and the generally blue and yellow plumage. Then my little friend did a vanishing act and disappeared into the pillar; I was more intrigued than ever. When he reappeared and flitted off again, I made a wonderful discovery. The blue tits had made their nest in the nook left behind by the stone. I stood and looked in wonder, the tiny space crammed with nestlings, their beaks agape as they hoped for more food. It was the most magical thing in the world to see them there; it was as if they were bringing the stones to life, filling them up with delight. One thing is certain: they filled my heart with joy for days afterwards. I marvelled not only at the resourcefulness of the parents in finding such a safe place for the nest, but also their devotion to their young. They were constantly coming and going. Sometimes they flitted in the branches of the ash, sometimes they clung acrobatically to the wrought iron curves of the gate, giving a few familiar calls before disappearing into the stone, and all the while the young were yellowing slowly, the mosses and feathers soft around them, their fabulous blue caps still missing. Nature is full of little secrets and surprises, things that could make us happy and give us hope if only we looked for them. When at last the young were fledged and the nest was empty I was sad and glad and full of wonder all at once.

Nature's ways are not always our ways though. I saw a hawk – a kestrel – snatch a songbird from the hedge and carry him off. I was sad, so sad for the songbird, but I marvelled too at the splendour of the kestrel with its reddish-brown upperparts, blue-grey head and tail and the stunning yellow legs. What happened seemed cruel to me, but this was the kestrel's way of sustaining his own magnificence and, like him or not, he is truly magnificent, especially in flight or in the act of hovering, his big pointed wings outspread, his fine grey tail like a fan.

There were beads of rain in the comfrey, the buds tubular and pink, drooping in clusters. I met a hare in the old boreen and almost at dark caught a glimpse of a badger down the road. The sight of his magical head, all black and white with stripes, filled me with delight. It was like reaching out and touching and holding the wild in my hands. Sometimes nature comes in the door to me. Last summer a wren flew in and played games of hide and seek. When I found her she was tucked away under the leaves of the lemon geranium that grew in an old clay pot. She looked such a picture there, the tiny little bird, the scented leaves around her, the pink flowers blooming too. In a while I took the pot and put it in the garden and my guest flew off again. The swallows have come back too. They are nesting in the shed again, the clematis by the door a mass of deep blue flowers. I was sitting at the table one day, the lazy tick of the clock filling the stillness, as the swallows came sweeping in through the open door. I looked with joy and delight as they fluttered and curled and curved under the oak brown boards of the high cathedral ceiling. This has been their practice of late: to fly into the house a few times every summer. Sometimes I think they know how much it means to me for I am always honoured by their coming. Looking up at them there made me feel close to you, dear friend, closer than ever. They filled me with wonder too, wonder at their spirit and courage. They come halfway round the world to find this place of old summers again; that is what we are to them, the place of old summer. Their coming into the house is like a kind of ritual, a blessing, a gift maybe. Whatever it is I am glad of it; it fills my heart with joy and delight.

Would anyone believe if I told them that on summer days I have lustre jugs and swallows and the tick of a drowsy clock? Sooty, my black labrador, threw a white eye at the swallows; he gave them a curious look, but then went back to sleep again. He knew that they meant him no harm. They did not stay very long and in a while I was standing at the door, watching them sweep into the brightness again; the sycamore weighed down with pinkish catkins, another sign of summer in the garden. I watch them dip and dive, the little blue-black birds; they were filling the skies with their song. They filled my heart with happy thoughts and even when I returned to my pen they were still in my mind. I began to think there was nothing more beautiful – more summery – than swallows and in time I followed their lead. I gave up my pen for the joys of the country lane. I went back to the thrushes and the foxgloves and the hart's-tongue ferns. And when the scent of woodbine gathered round me I was like one drinking summer again.

Until I write again,

Always your friend,

Patrick

JULY

I have been to a cottage, an old mountain cottage that I have known before, the gentle murmur of a stream nearby. There were no more roses anymore, but there were huge clumps of lilies still, arum lilies by the door. They spring to life every summer and it was lovely to see them again. Some had even seeded themselves among the crags in the stream, their majestic funnel-shaped flowers and big green leaves a magical sight, the stream tumbling gently down and down again to the lake far below. The lilies were magnificent, the hedgerows of fuchsia around them radiant too. Sometimes I wonder what the honey bees would do without the fuchsia bells; it was as if they were made for each other. The fuchsia bells have a splendour of their own, silky reds and purples shining in the drowsy afternoon. I love the humming of the honey-bees; the very sound of them fills me with pleasure, but there is another sound that I love too.

I walked with my niece Eleanor and her little daughter Caoimhe around the road to the little country bridge. Caoimhe had buttercups like stars in her hair. Her mother gave her a kiss and called her a princess. We left the road and stood in the long, lush grasses by the stream, the water dark and bright, bubbling over stones. The water had a brownish peaty tinge and yet so clear that every stone could be seen below. Every stone was a different colour. The music of the stream was magical. It made me think how nice it would be to lie down like a child for a while in the warm grasses and fall asleep, just listening to the soft sounds of the stream. It was not just the water that was making music, but the stones and the mountain and you, dear friend, the very earth itself, all in celebration of the glorious summer day. The sky was blue, the clouds like candyfloss on the tops of the mountains. It was a magical feeling, listening to the stream and watching it bubble under the bridge, then making soft meanders, twisting and turning and curving through the grasses and the bogs. It was as if it had all the time in the world, as if it were in no great hurry at all. I wondered why we are always in a hurry. We are always coming and going, running here and there and back again, as if our lives depended on it and then when we look back we wonder why. What was the meaning of it all?

I looked up, following the line of the stream back up the mountain. I could not pick out its source, but it was enough to know that it was there, nestled somewhere in the crags and shining in the light. I thought of it as a magic place, a wellspring of music and beauty, a storehouse of tunes for a summer's day. There were sheep on the mountain and wild goats too, making little of the crags and the sharp inclines. It was as if nature were a book and we had come to the most beautiful page, a page full of colours and sounds and softness. We lingered a long time by the stream, reluctant to leave its music behind. I have seen orchids here in early summer, wild orchids growing in the damp mosses and bogs. And rarer still the hooded deep blue flowers of the butterwort, the yellow leaves curled at the edges. The orchids and the butterwort were gone for another year but the rushes were in flower. I love the flowers of the rushes as much as I love any plant. They too are part of the magic of summer. We found a shining rock pool by the stream and in it the glitter of tiny fishes, flitting and flashing and shining like silver. No little corner but does not have life of its own. Caoimhe, the buttercup princess, is only three or four and had to be carried most of the way home. She insisted, however, on walking up the hill before us, her walking so purposeful, so full of intent we said she looked like a woman going home to feed her ducks or maybe to bake bread.

There is another magical place that I want to tell you about, dear friend. It is just an old damp meadow left undisturbed by time. Sometimes I call it the

corncrake meadow because it has echoes of all those little meadows where the corncrake nested years ago, the kind that were mowed with a scythe, the hay tossed and turned with pitchforks or with curious horse-drawn contraptions called 'tumblers'. The corncrake meadow teems with all kinds of magical things: masses and masses of glorious yellow flags, the magnificent yellow flowers set among stiff, green sword-shaped leaves. Then there is the reedmace with their fruiting spikes, dark velvety brown in colour, soft, so soft to the touch. Here too are little thickets of meadowsweet, one of the joys of summer. The frothy heads of creamy white flowers filling the air with their delicious scent, the scent still drowsier, heavier in the lazy afternoon. And grazing among the flags and the reedmace are two horses, one white, the other piebald. There is nothing statuesque about them, nothing of the flowing lines of the thoroughbred and yet they have an inherent dignity of their own, a dignity born and bred of the marsh, of years and years in the rushes and grasses and meadowsweet, not just themselves, I mean, but all of their line before them. I don't know what it is about them, but they fill me with contentment. When I stop and look at them they make me feel good inside. I am happy to be me: I don't need to be anyone else.

I have seen the white horse standing and grazing, the piebald resting beside her. There is such a feeling of stillness about them, a feeling of stillness and quiet. They, like the stream, know the value of simple things. They are in no great hurry at all; they are making the most of summer. If I could put into words how they make me feel, I think I would be a very good poet.

There are times when I long to stand in the marsh beside them, but I never do. They are my magic and I do not want to break the spell. If I were a painter, I would paint them and put them in a picture on my wall, but maybe it is better this way. They are always painting pictures in my head.

I must tell you too of the blackbirds in the cherry trees by the river. There is nothing more beautiful than a yellow-billed blackbird with a cherry in his mouth, the leaves all bright and green around him. You were the one who gave him this river garden and I know that he is glad of it. The graceful white flowers of April and May have given way again to the bright red cherries and the blackbird is full of joy. I love all the green leaves of high summer, the overhanging boughs making arbours of their own down leafy lanes and roads. Sometimes I stand like a child and look up through the leaves and boughs, the sunlight winking and flashing and gleaming, as though playing games for summer. I hope, dear earth, that I will never take all of this beauty for granted, and as I stand here looking up, grant me one wish: let me always see summer through the eyes of a child.

Until I write again,

Always your friend,

Patrick

AUGUST

Dear Earth,

I love the old church by the sea, especially the angels that decorate the walls by the altar. The angels are small, but beautifully carved and coloured, and I have always liked such things. The old church by the sea is a haven of quiet. On a quiet summer's day you can hear the stillness in every part, the sunlight glinting and glancing in the stained glass windows behind the altar. I left the church behind and there before me was the splendour of the sea, blue and bright and shining, the old clock tower by the pier painted in deep sienna and white. The sea has always touched the soul, the spirit, the imagining of the Irish. It is hardly surprising I suppose, for we are an island people. Nothing is more certain about the Celts than that they believed in the things of the spirit. They believed in an otherworld beyond the sea, an island haven of harmony and peace. They called it Mag Mell, the Plain of Delight, Tir Tairngiri, the Land of Promise, Tir na nÓg, the Land of Youth. The privileged few undertook *imrama* or voyages to this fabled place, their voyages described by a succession of lyric poets, including monastic poets. The natural beauty of the place was celebrated, the trees and flowers and birds, the latter brightly plumaged and lulling everyone to sleep with their beautiful music. It was a place of simple but sensuous pleasures: the beauty of groves and blossoms, the taste of the wild berries and fruits, the silvered promise of waters in sacred wells and fountains, the blue waves lapping the shore. The sea is still a place of imagining for me, a place of fishes and colours and shells, of boats and anchors and sails, of mysteries as old as time itself. The lighthouse stood upon the rocks in the far distance, gleaming in the sunlight. I thought to myself what a wonderful, welcoming sight it must be to sailors tossed on the tide, the brightness of its beams filling the dark. Among the boats was a lifeboat. Glitters of light in the sea were reflected in its dark blue hull. They looked like star showers there, dazzling and gleaming and shining.

Gulls came and went from the pier, but those that settled there for a while had the look of old fishermen about them. It was as if they knew every part of the sea and it knew them, as if they were lost in reflections of their own. There were herring gulls, their heads and underparts white, their backs and wings lightly grey, their legs pink. The great black-backed gulls looked bigger, their heads and underparts white too, but their backs and wings much darker. There too were a few mottled brown young of both species, the sea blue and green and shining. What could be more beautiful than to sit by the sea on a sunny afternoon, to stop and think awhile, visiting islands again, islands of imagining; to give a place to beauty in our lives, nurturing the senses with the wonders of the tide, ripples and waves and shimmers of light, brightness everywhere, celebrating too the stillness of another summer's day. There were boats at anchor here and there; many were fibreglass, some with sails, but a few traditional fishing boats too. I thought of the boats as emblems, emblems of man's communion with the sea, whether fishing for his livelihood, or boating for pleasure or rejoicing in the rhythm of the stroke, the pulse of the oars on regatta day. I looked up at the seagulls and marvelled at their soaring overhead. I have often seen them following in the wake of a fishing boat, hoping for gifts of silver, but they are truly majestic in flight. They soar and circle, then circle and soar again, their movements unhurried, graceful but wonderfully powerful too. Sometimes they spread their wings and glide on the updrafts of air, when they seem more graceful still. I wondered what it would be like to be like them looking down on the jewelled sea, the royal blue giving way to a greenish jade far out from the shore.

So much of your surface, dear earth, is covered

with the beauty of the sea. Time and again it has healed and renewed itself in the face of oil spills and slicks and damaged coastlines, but we have to show it respect, to give it the place of honour it deserves. Anyone who looks at the sea, whether they feel lonely, forgotten, or maybe just sad at heart, cannot but be moved by its beauty, touched by its spirit of wildness and grandeur. As I stood and watched the boats and the gulls, the briny smell in the air, I thought of the far places, the distant shores lapped by the sea, the teeming shoals of fishes, the strangeness and beauty that I could only imagine. I was glad of my imagining, I was glad of the sea and just around the coast a dolphin was dancing in the sun. As I walked the little road by the church, I saw the yellow vetchlings and trefoils tossing by the wayside. More than anything else, however, there were great sweeps of montbretia, orange in the grasses. Another name for montbretia is crocosmia, a name which means 'fragrance of crocuses'. When the bulbs were put into the water they were found to have a scent of saffron, just like the bulbs of the crocus. I love waste places, little bits of wild left to their own devices, nettles and thistles for butterflies and finches, the purple of the knapweeds vying with the thistle tops, spires of loosestrife purpling too and glorious meadow cranesbills bluer than the sea.

Not so long ago someone stopped me on the street and told me of a poem she learned at school. 'The Time that Timothy Lost' tells of a boy on his way to school: he loses time when he stops to admire the little things of nature along the way. One of the lines of the poem describes him stopping to admire the beauty of the linnet's nest. *An gleoiseach* is the Irish name for the linnet while its Latin name is *carduelis cannabina*. Linnets are not nearly as colourful as other finches, but the breeding male has a patch of red on his forehead and upper breast in summer, the female duller and browner. There is nothing lovelier than to hear the linnet sing in the yellow sweeps of gorse. If any song was made for summer it is the linnet's. The song of the male is not only musical, but also sustained; that magical song and the scent of the gorse are among the joys of summer days. Those who are observant can pick out the male singing on top of a yellow spray. He does not seem to mind in the least the prickly spikes all round him, the fine yellow blooms brighter still in the sun. The linnet's nesting season extends from April to August, the best of moss lined with wool or hair or down, the eggs pale blue with reddish brown markings. Like all finches, linnets love seed-bearing weeds but the use and overuse of herbicides have had adverse consequences for birds such as the linnet. Where they have survived at all, the wild flowers have largely been banished to the margins and headlands or to waste ground. The protection of these wild places is a small price to pay for the magical song of the linnet. No wonder then that Timothy stopped to admire the beauty of the linnet's nest. Maybe in a way, it told him more than he could ever find in books.

Here too among the heathers and the gorse I have heard the jingle-jangle of the stonechats. The latter, jaunty, lively little birds have long been favourites of mine. The male is very colourful with his orange breast, dark head and white neck patch, the female duller and browner.

Nature still has islands of quiet in the summer, places by the sea or among the heathers. Thank you, dear Earth, for the stillness of summer days, the blue and green of the tide, the flowers dabbling colour in the margins. We are no more than your keepers for you have been given to us in trust. Let us cherish and protect all that is wild and beautiful, passing it on unspoiled to those who come after us. Let us give thanks and celebrate diversity: frogs and ladybirds and roses in the garden. May we never become so acquisitive that we begin to lose sight of such things, remembering still the gentle power of beauty. We are all the richer for it, for the colour it brings to our lives.

Until I write again,

Always your friend,

Patrick

SEPTEMBER

Dear Earth,
The summer is over and the children are going back to school again. I was thinking of the boys that I met on the road one day. Two of them I knew well; they were neighbours of mine, but their two friends were strangers to me. I had not seen them before. All four were on the way to the river with the dogs. There was nothing the dogs liked better than to swim in the river on long hot summer days. The two newcomers were fair-haired, aged about ten or eleven and very friendly with the dogs, patting them and stroking them and repeating their names with a kind of relish. They looked like happy children – bright, good-humoured and full of life. Their names were Victor and Vadzim, all the way from a faraway place, Belarus. Like many people, I knew little or nothing about Belarus before the explosion there made international news. It was strange to think that the two boys were living there, that they had come to Ireland for a short holiday. They did not speak our language and we did not speak theirs and yet they

seemed perfectly content. They knew that they were welcome. One of them even indulged in a bit of playful jostling with his new friends. It was as if friendship had a language of its own, a language that had no need of words. When they said goodbye, I was still lost in thought. It was sad to think that their home place was so contaminated. Everything wholesome made unwholesome, everything beautiful laid to waste. It was as if the two boys, and more besides, had been deprived of their inheritance, the beauty of earth, the bounty of rivers, the wonder of all things green and growing. All of these had been taken from them and I wondered why it happened, why it was allowed to happen. Why did we put our faith in such destructive technologies, when we knew that we were putting at risk our treasure of treasures, our riches of riches, the very fabric of the earth itself, your fabric, dear friend, the very thing that sustains not just us but all living things on this beautiful planet?

It was like a man with a jewel putting it in the way of thieves. If we have learned anything from Chernobyl it is that we cannot live apart from nature, we cannot be separate from it. We cannot survive without the survival of all that is good and beautiful on earth and in this context at least the words 'good' and 'beautiful' go together hand in hand just as their opposites do. Pollution and plunder are one and the same, especially pollution on such a devastating scale as this. It is no more than a plundering of the riches that rightly belong to those who come after us. I saw a cobweb shining in the garden. It made me think that we are all part of the one planet, the one earth: we are all threads in the web of life. What happens in one part matters to us all. Chernobyl could and should have been a watershed in our thinking and yet strangely it seems that we are happy enough to go on as before.

It serves no purpose, however, to complain of global wrongs if we are not troubled by the sight of litter in bogs and groves and waterways. No-one would think of throwing rubbish in their own garden and that is why I wish we would think of the world as a garden, a beautiful garden to be shared by us all. Victor and Vadzim and their friends were glad of the river and I could only wish that there would always be rivers like this, shining channels of water to revive the spirit and give it hope.

There were butterflies and blackberries in the hedges. There were tortoiseshells all summer long but then there were peacocks and red admirals too. The beautiful red admirals do not survive the winter here but every spring there is a northward migration from the Mediterranean. It is the offspring of these butterflies which bring such colour to our autumn hedges. The taste of the blackberries was deliciously sweet and wild, evocative as it was of all the goodness of earth, your goodness, dear friend. No one tends the blackberries, no one cossets them or make a fuss about them and still they flower and fruit and fill the hedges with delight. The flowers of the blackberry, panicles of white, tinged with pink or violet, are remarkably beautiful and it is a pity that more is not thought of them. Their fruits too are undervalued.

Plentiful, accessible, with a taste that speaks of the hedge and the rain and the morning dew.

The pigeons meanwhile were making a feast of the elderberries that hung in clusters here and there. It was lovely, not only to see them, but to hear them flap and flutter round the berries. While the overall appearance is one of soft grey plumage, closer views of the birds reveal sheens of green and pink on the head and breast with a white mark on the sides of the neck. Pigeons not only love berries and nuts, such as acorns and beechmast, they also eat seeds and grain. Their coos, soft and throaty, sound especially content at this time of year when seeds and fruits are at their most plentiful. It was easy to sense their delight with the elderberries and I had the feeling they knew what was good for them. Elderberries have, of course, long been part of Irish folk medicine, used in the making of wine, preserves and compotes. The spiny green fruits of the horse-chestnut begin to open to reveal their contents, the familiar chestnuts. The rich brown of the chestnuts is beautifully autumnal in tone, bringing to fulfillment the promise of the flowery spikes of April and May. Harbingers too of yellow leaves and all the glowing days of autumn, the chestnuts have echoes of childhood games and innocence.

Emhain Abhlack, Emhain of the Apple Trees, was one of the names given by the Celts to their fabled Otherworld. I have just two old apple trees but there is nothing lovelier than to climb the ladder and pick the fruits from the branches. The scent of the leaves and the boughs is delicious, the smoothness of the fruits marvellous too. It was as if the soft apple green of the leaves gathered round me, as if I were part of some magical voyage. It was easy to see why the Celts gave the apple tree a place of honour in their island paradise. The rowan tree more than any other was the tree of the druids; however, druids such as Trosdan, Cabadius, Tages, Dadera and Lamhderg. Even their very names have a kind of resonance. Two of the most famous druids of all, however, were Cathbadh, who predicted trouble at the birth of Deirdre, and Mogh Rath who rowed the wheel of the sun and who lived on Oilean Dairbhre, Valentia Island. It was on wattles of rowan that the druids slept in order to see into the future. Much of what has been written about them suggests a sense of wonder at the things of nature.

I sensed something of that wonder too when I came to the old stones, the sky to the east streaked with crimson in the still of the morning. The stillness was so deep, so real I could almost reach out and touch it and hold it in my hand. The touch of the stones too was magical: it was in a way like a bridge to the past. The stones were commemorative, marked as they were with the familiar lines of the old Irish ogham script. I did not understand the script, but like my encounter with the boys it hardly seemed to matter. The stones spoke to me in other ways: they spoke to the senses and the spirit; they spoke the language of the heart. Statements of art and expression, they gave voice to a longing for remembrance. 'Remember us; we have passed this way too', they seemed to say, and indeed those they recalled were renowned for a great many things: their belief in the things of the spirit, their reverence for woods and groves and streams, the dwelling places of so many of their deities, their celebration of all the things of nature in their wonderful tales and sagas. Nature was their sustainer, their source of imagining too, a creative force in their lives. It made me wonder what our times will be remembered for: depletion of natural resources, pollution of earth, sea and sky, divisions between north and south, rich and poor. Hopefully not. As I stood and looked at the stones I thought again of the ancients who put them there. Although we are separated by time we are not so different from them. We too have a need for quiet and colour in our lives. We too can bring our dreams to the river and look for fulfilment there. I thought of the two young boys, the boys from a far place. I wished them well on their return to school and I hoped they took home something of the spirit of the river with them: the beauty, the brightness, the courage, the hope. I was glad of the stillness, the sun soft and crimson, spilling light in the east. Creation made new in the first breath of morning. I was glad of the stones, speaking in voices that only the spirit could hear.

Until I write again,

Always your friend,

Patrick

OCTOBER

Dear Earth,

I remember reading a book written by a woman years ago. When I first took it up, I wasn't sure if I would be able to relate to it or not. After all it was written so long before, not just in a different country, but a different world. So much had changed in the interval. I have to admit there were passages I found difficult, but the one thing I could readily identify with was the love of nature. There was respect for trees and flowers and birds, for all the wonders of creation. There was the sense that nothing was ordinary, everything beautiful, special in its own way. A huge framed picture of the woman who wrote the book hung in our house for years. It was given to my grandmother by a neighbour of hers. The name of the woman in the picture was St Thérèse of Lisieux. When her relics came to Ireland I went to see them. As I stood in line I wondered what St Thérèse would have liked most about the scene: the queues, the grand cathedral or maybe the fabulous tree in the cathedral grounds. I decided on the tree. It looked magnificent in the evening light.

I couldn't imagine a world without trees. They are the essence of beauty, nature's living art and architecture. They are splendour of bole and branch and bud and leaf, flowers that blossom and fruits that fall in due season. They are storytellers too. They tell the story of the passing year, from the leafy greens of spring and summer to the yellow glory of the fall. They have the music of seasons in them: daffodils and bluebells, roses and ragwort, the rhythms of sun and rain, the gleam of snow on distant hills. They embody all that is good and beautiful in nature's cycle, the circles of the years going round, circles remembered in the rings of the trees themselves. They are the memory keepers, the living witnesses to the past. In long lived trees such as oak, the weather patterns can be traced back for hundreds of years, into periods for which no records of any kind exist. Whether they stand alone or gather together in groves, there is something magical that draws us to them. Even in winter, the evergreens serve as a foil for the wonderful tracery of their deciduous neighbours. Trees create a sense of permanence in the landscape. It is as if they or their ancestors have always been here and will always be here. Many of them have been seen by fathers and grandfathers and great grandfathers too. In that way they are a very real link with those who have gone before. They are the singing stalls of birds: blackbirds, thrushes, robins, fluting, piping, warbling. Melodies for spring and summer, some for autumn too. Our world is full of noise: the restless drone of cars and lorries, the impatient honking of horns, even the bland background music in the supermarket, music that is meant to soothe and cajole and make us amenable to buying more. Despite all of this, however, there is still a deep reservoir of quiet at the very heart of nature, and nowhere is that quiet, that stillness, more tangible than in the woods and groves. I have walked in different woods, but the feeling is in them all, the feeling of quiet and calm and peace.

There is a wood that follows the contours of a mountain rising higher and higher still. The path climbs steeply at first, before levelling off and then running parallel with the road below though the road is not seen. There are a great many pines in the wood, the air deliciously green and scented, especially after rain. Some of their trunks are green with moss, wonderfully soft to the touch. There are mosses and ferns and wood sorrel everywhere in summer. The path is fringed with deciduous trees, rowans bright with berries, the arching boughs of the larch, their needles soft and green, turning yellow in the fall. Sometimes the branches are beaded with rain when they create a magic of their own, birch trees too, their thin peeling bark a familiar feature. I met an old man one time whose family were 'keepers of the wood' for generations. Talking to him made me aware of the social importance of trees. The old oak wood was cut down in famine times and replaced with larch as a relief measure to give employment. The larch wood in turn was cut down during the First World War, the timber used to provide pit props for the trenches in France. Happily the wood was replanted again and still thrives to this very day, all of which illustrates the enduring bond between man and grove. The old man also recalled the forestry horses at work. They were broad-shouldered, placid, gentle, and when he spoke of them I heard the affection in his voice.

Rushing has become such a part of our lives it is almost like second nature to us now. We accept it as part of the human condition. Just take a look at the streets of any busy town or city. There are some who would say it is the disease of our times. And then we complain that we have no time anymore, but it's all about choices, isn't it? We are all free agents. We make our own choices, our own decisions. We don't have to follow the flock. We don't have to accept the spin of the marketing men if we don't want to. Consumerism is all about making the superfluous seem essential, about creating a demand where none exists. It sets no boundaries. The notion of being content with enough alien to it. No-one has enough anymore in this consumer age.

The mountain wood echoes with the sound of water. The stream flows down from a great height, the gradient so steep that sometimes in autumn it takes on the character of a waterfall. There is no thought of rushing here. Then there is all that light and shadow too, sunlight, spilling, sprinkling, dancing, dripping, pouring through the wild greens overhead. One day as we sat on a bench, Sooty lying on the ground before us, I noticed a branch move across the way. The movement intrigued me as I heard no flutter of wings. I wondered if it might be a squirrel. We were coming to the wood a very long time but we never saw one. A few moments later the riddle was solved. We were walking along again when a squirrel darted across the path before us, then scurried up the trunk of a huge old pine. He filled me with joy and delight, the handsome red squirrel. It was lovely to see him sitting in the branches in the bright morning sun. He looked such a picture there. Wealth and display of wealth are equated with success and happiness today. Such ideas are foisted on on us time and again by large sections of the media. The rich and the famous are the icons of our time. We read about their homes, their cars, their holidays, their lifestyle. I have to confess I would rather be looking at squirrels in branches. I don't know if he knows but I think he would make a very good philosopher, the little red squirrel. He tells me that there is more than one kind of success, that happiness doesn't always come with riches. Happiness is found in the wild and wooded places where blackbirds flute and thrushes sing. Here there are riches for the spirit and nature provides for her own.

Those who lived in the age of the half door would have said that time was more than money. It was friendship, companionship, a chat with the neighbours, a sense of community too. Even the clocks that ticked in the background, old-fashioned wall clocks, gingerbread and steeple clocks had a homelier, more leisurely feel about them, as if they approved of the notion that time was for sharing.

It is in the fall that the handsome beech trees come into their own. It is then that their glossy green leaves give way to marvellous tints, yellow and gold and russet red, crimson and tawny and flame. The beech trees flank the road and it is almost as if the sun is mesmerised by the wonderful surge of colour, as if it is playing games with the leaves. The trees begin to drowse and fall asleep, their leaves tumbling in clouds, their cycle complete for another year. I am glad of the beauty of the beech trees, dear friend, their splendour in the sun. Seeing them there in the light I have all the riches I need. I am happy with my lot.

Until I write again,

Always your friend,

Patrick

NOVEMBER

Dear Earth,

November is the month of the dark, they say. The days are getting shorter and the nights are drawing in. In the old Celtic world, 1 November was the feast of Samhain, which marked the end of summer and the beginning of winter. Of all the Celtic festivals, Samhain was by far the most important. The eve of Samhain marked the border between winter and summer. It was in many senses time out of time and so was charged with supernatural force. Then the fairy mounds were thrown open and the people of the *sidh*, the fairy race, as well as the spirits of the dead, made contact with the living. The feast was closely associated with the dying back of nature and there were ceremonies in honour of the gods of the harvest. If the spirits came to visit the human world, however, then humankind might equally visit theirs. Most accounts of such visits took the form of wonderful voyages, but the mounds were also accessible by cave, especially at Samhain. One of the most famous caves of them all was Uaimh Cruachan, near the royal fortress of Ailill and Medbh, king and queen of Connaught. One of those who visited the otherworld through the cave was Nera. Part of his story again illustrates the association of Samhain with the coming of winter. Nera had many strange adventures inside the *sidh*, amongst them a vision of the royal fortress of Cruachan in flames. He determines to return to bring warning to his own people, bringing with him the fruits of summer, wild garlic and primrose and golden fern as proofs of his story. If Samhain was the beginning of winter in the human world, then it was always summer amongst the spirits and the gods.

The thrush can be heard singing in November. More often than not, these are young birds getting in a bit of practice for the coming of spring. Their song is wild, melodious and bright, all the more so as winter draws nigh. Still for all that it is the easiest thing in the world to feel something of the gathering gloom in winter. The trees are leafless, bare, the hedges tangled, the skies oppressively grey. It is as if the light is fading and the dark is gaining sway. I don't know why, but I felt something of the dark inside me last year. I found no pleasure in the trees or birds or the grey tide swelling. It was almost as if they were strangers to me and I was the same to them. I began to think I had lost my feeling for them and that was the worst thought of all. They were the things that gave me the strength and courage and hope, the things that gave meaning to life. Deep down I suppose I knew that they were no less beautiful than they ever were. I was the one who changed. I had known the dark before, but it was so long ago I had almost forgotten the colour of it.

The greenfinches were making the most of rosehips in the garden, the rich orange glow of the hips shining in their bills for only a moment. I loved to see them there but still the sadness did not leave me. Even the thought of pleasures past, of woods and streams and leafy lanes, brought me no joy: they were but vague, half-remembered things so that I found myself longing for the sun time and time again. There were days when it seemed as if it would never come, but then one day out of the blue it came to me at last; a gift of a day, with clear blue skies and brilliant sunshine, a day to rival any that summer gave.

There were diamonds of light in the river, all gleaming and flashing and shining, making glitters everywhere. Even the mountains were seen in soft reflex below, so that it was hard to tell what was real and what was not. I could not resist the impulse to go for a walk by the river and as I walked along the shelduck rose and skimmed across the tide with their loud quacking calls. I like the shelduck: they are full of life and colour. Their heads are glossy green, their bills red and their legs pink. There is something lovely about them: it is almost as if someone decided to paint them one colour and then changed their mind as they went along. Not only that, they are very much part of the scene: I could not imagine the place without them. They make their nests in the old sandstone cliffs, making use of rabbits' burrows where they find them. In many places the young, accompanied by their parents, have to cover long distances to get to water, but not so here. They are close to the river's edge. Very often young birds form a crèche in the care of an adult. All of this happens in summer, of course, but it was lovely to hear their calls that bright November day.

As I walked along I saw the old stone cabin in the distance. There was a time years ago when it was used by the bailiffs keeping watch on the river. There too was the big grey rock hugging the rivers edge. It is a favourite with the cormorants when they come ashore to dry their wings. They are a familiar sight standing on the rock, their big black wings outspread, but they were not there then. I walked on a little further and then it happened. A stranger appeared out of nowhere. It was almost as if he came out of the rock itself. He stopped me in my tracks: I looked at him in wonder. I stood quite still and watched him, a handsome red fox by the river, his rich red coat aglow in the bright November sun. He was like a bit of magic, all the more lovely for being so unexpected. He was standing still too, looking in my direction, but as I made no move he did not turn and run away.

I have always loved foxes ever since I was a child. We caught a glimpse of one now and then in the grove and there was something about them, something elusive, mysterious, beautiful. I sensed it again when I looked at the river fox. He had a kind of wildness about him, the wildness of woods and groves and secret trails. There was something of the fairytale about him too: it was as if he had just stepped out of a storybook. I don't know how long we stood looking at each other, myself and the river fox, but it was long enough. The old sandstone cliffs were warm in the sun, the tide was brimming and bright and the shelduck had come to rest across the way. Still, all I could think of was the fox. I was willing him to stay longer and longer again. I did not want him to leave.

It was as if the sun were playing games with his coat, making it shine more brightly still. If I tried to imagine him, I could not have made him more wonderful. He filled me with delight and intrigue. I wondered what brought him to the river on such a beautiful day, but then maybe just like me he was glad of the brightness too. I don't know what it was about him that touched me so deeply: his wildness, his beauty, the strangeness of his coming, but one thing was certain; he was the brightness for me. And the feelings of dark that stalked me before made him all the more welcome, all the more wonderful still.

I stood spellbound by him all the while. I longed to reach out and touch him and stroke him, but of course I knew it could not happen and maybe in a way it was better that way. He was still a mystery to me, still elusive, out of reach. It was not every day that I encountered such beauty and when he turned at last he did so at his leisure. There was nothing anxious, hurried about him: he sauntered away at his ease. He felt at home by the river. It was more than familiar to him. I was glad, so glad of our encounter. It made me happy not just for the rest of the day, but for a long time afterwards. I still pictured him by the brimming silver of the river. I thought of the day as a gift, a gift of wonder. Dear earth, thank you for the fox and the river and the light, for reminding me that nature inspires not just in the moment but in the memory of it afterwards. That was how it was with me and the fox. He was my brightness, my joy by shining water, a joy that lives in memory still.

Until I write again,

Always your friend,

Patrick

DECEMBER

Dear Earth,

Someone once wrote that candles were like little pools of light in the darkness of a northern winter; the same could be said of the robin's song, I think. It too is a little pool of light in the dark of the year. An old Victorian bird book describes the robin as 'the favourite of children' and there was a time when bird nesting was a popular children's past-time. It was the loveliest thing in the world to come upon a robin's nest in a mossy bank, or hollow tree, even in an old abandoned kettle somewhere in a hedge. The little white eggs with their light red spots inspired a sense of wonder too, which helps to explain why the robin's nest was the most cherished of all.

Robins are fiercely territorial and this is one of the main reasons why they sing at all, to announce their territory to would-be rivals of their own kind. This instinct is particularly strong in springtime, when there are regular skirmishes, but it is also prevalent in winter, when both male and female sing. It is magical to hear them at their song among the bare branches, their lovely red breasts caught in the bright crisp glow of the sun. The poet WH Davies wrote:

> Robin on a leafless bough,
> Lord in heaven how he sings
> Now cold winters cruel wind
> Makes playmates of poor dead things.

The robin's Christian associations meant that it was especially revered, it's nest the most cherished of all. As William Wordsworth wrote:

> Art thou the bird whom man loves best,
> the pious bird with the scarlet breast.

The lines also underline the robin's affinity with man and there are very few gardeners who have not had the pleasure of seeing a robin perched on a pitchfork at one time or another. The robin has a cheeky but loveable gait, what the ornithologist Nicholson referred to as 'an engaging boldness', the head being cocked alertly to bring to bear one or other of 'the bright beady eyes'.

In Irish tradition, the robin was particularly associated with the O'Sullivan family, being known as 'spideog Mhuintir Ui Shuileabháin'. Another Irish adage praised the courage of the robin, perhaps because it continues to sing in winter when most of its counterparts are silent. The quality of the song changes, of course, after the summer moult, but it is as if the robin knows that winter will not last. The robin's red breast also explains its popularity at Christmas, its rufous plumage a striking contrast to the bleakness of winter snows. The poet Anthony Rye captured the image very well when he wrote that 'the red breast smoulders in the waste of snow.' Of course, it was the Victorians who made the robin a Christmas card favourite. One lovely old card, published in the 1880s has the rhyme:

> Little robin redbreast to the window comes,
> seeking warmth and shelter, asking us for crumbs.
> Shall we not remember all outside our door,
> whom the chill December finds hungry, sad and poor?

Thus the underlying message was one of kindliness and goodness at Christmas time. I have my own robin friend. Autumn mornings found him perched at the very top of the kalmia outside my kitchen window, the sky to the east painted with orange. He did not seem to mind that the showy clusters of flowers had long since faded, a great mass of glossy green leaves all around him. He had reasons to sing and it was nice to think that he was singing to me.

I was walking by the river one day when I thought I caught sight of a jewel. It was only the briefest of glimpses but it filled me with delight. The kingfisher is surely one of the most beautiful of all the river birds. It is fond of large, slow-moving rivers, though it may also haunt smaller streams and ponds, and is found in estuaries near the coast in winter. The head and wings are blue, or greenish-blue, depending on the light, mottled lightly on the crown and the coverts of the wings. The back is a brilliant azure blue, the throat and the sides of the neck white, the underparts rich chestnut or orange. When the bird is at rest, however, it is not always easy to pick him out. Then the darker wings cover the azure blue of the back and the underparts blend in with the background, especially with the leaves in autumn. The long pointed beak looks half as long as the whole bird, giving him a characteristic wedge-shaped appearance. When he is seen at all, it is generally in flight, skimming low and straight over water, his blue wings beating rapidly.

The kingfisher needs not only clean water for fishes but high sandy banks for nesting. It is in these that the nest is made, the tunnel sloping upwards to the nest site. The eggs which number six to eight are glossy white and when the young are hatched in about three weeks, they are fed on regurgitated fish, a mass of fish bones gathering round them. All of this takes place in summer but there are echoes of it still in winter. It is then on misty winter days that the sheer blue brilliance of the bird seems more magical than ever. Its shrill call, a bright 'chee', frequently repeated, echoes too. Nothing could be more lovely than to see that electric blue flash along the estuary and to hear the wild delighted call. It is like reaching out and touching the wild, if only for a moment;

> It was the Rainbow gave thee birth,
> and left thee all her lovely hues,
> And as her mother's name was Tears,
> so runs it in thy blood to choose,
> For haunts the lonely pools,
> and keep in company with trees that weep.
>
> *WH Davies*

There are always swans on the river but they look especially beautiful when the snowy peaks are white and gleaming. They have a kind of mystery about them then. It is no great wonder that they figure so prominently in Irish myth and legend, not just in the story of the Children of Lir, but in other tales too. In the Wooing of Etain, the god Midir comes to Tara to claim the beautiful Etain as his own. 'He put his right hand around Etain and bore her up through the skylight of the house. Ashamed, the hosts rose up around the king, and they saw the two swans circling high over Tara before flying off to Midir's home.' Yeats was just one of many of a later generation of poets who celebrated the beauty of swans. He saw them as symbols, not just of love and companionship, but also of creativity, and most of all, of immortality. The swans I saw on the river had that feeling about them too, the feeling of timelessness, as if they and their kind would go on and on forever.

A few years ago it rained all day on Christmas Eve, the wind blowing strongly too. It was well after dusk before the rain cleared and the wind abated at last. Still, late as it was I could not resist the impulse to go back to the river. There I stood on the bank watching the tide awhile. The tide was high and grey and restless, swollen with rain and flood. Across the darkened bay there were lights in every window. Twinkling and gleaming and shining, they looked like the scatterings of stars. I remember thinking how beautiful it was: the bay and the lights and the restless swell. More than that, there was something wonderfully lonely and strong about the tide, a loneliness that soothed the spirit and made it glad. It was the kind of scene that made me want to wish again, wish that such beauty would never fade but would go on and on forever. It filled me with imagining, the swelling of the tide like music in my ears for every season has music of its own. I remember feeling happy, so happy as I made my way home through the fields, then lighting my candle and placing it in my window.

The mountains were white in the morning and the bells were ringing crisp and clear across the river. There is nothing lovelier than the sound of bells over water. It is lovely to hear them at any time of year, but especially so at Christmas. Sound and silver mingling together, becoming as one in the magic of Christmas morning. There were showers of hail but when the sun came out it shone resplendent in the water, dazzling too in the snowy peaks that seemed to touch the sky. If I tried to imagine anything more beautiful, I could not have done so.

Dear earth, inspire us with your beauty, the wonder of woods and groves, cliffs and stars and shining seas, the birds at their song. Help us to celebrate nature, to cherish its wonderful gifts, sharing them with all who share the planet with us.

Until I write again,
Always your friend,

Patrick